No Apples in Eden:
New and Selected Poems

Acknowledgements:

Many thanks to Bogle-L'Ouverture for permission to reprint poems from *Lure of the Cascadura (1989)*.

Thanks also to the editors of the following publications in which some of these poems appeared:

Ambit
Bogle L'Ouverture
Crocus Books
First Draft
Hansib Publications
The North
Paladin Poetry
Poetry Matters
Poetry Review
Stride

No Apples in Eden:
New and Selected Poems

For Maggie, John Lyons

Best wishes and future success
30/4/2011

Smith/Doorstop Books

Published 2009 by
Smith/Doorstop Books
The Poetry Business
Bank Street Arts
32-40 Bank Street
Sheffield S1 2DS

Copyright © John Lyons 2009
All Rights Reserved

ISBN 978-1-902382-99-9

British Library Cataloguing-in-Publication Data. A
catalogue record for this book is available from the
British Library.

Typeset at The Poetry Business
Printed by Lightning Source
Cover: detail from 'Carnival Jourvay' by John Lyons
Photograph of the author by Jean Rees

Distributed by Central Books Ltd., 99 Wallis Road,
London E9 5LN

The Poetry Business gratefully acknowledges
financial assistance of Arts Council England.

Supported by
ARTS COUNCIL
ENGLAND

For my wife, Jean
and my sons, Cyril, Edouard, Guillaume and Antoine

CONTENTS

The Sun Rises In The North

Behind the Carnival

Voices From A Silk-Cotton Tree

New Poems

A GRANDMOTHER'S HOME RULE

1

He lived anxious days of learning
under his grandmother's stern eye,
leather strap, her fierce faith in English:
Des days in dis island people tink dey free.
Dey callit ee man cee pay shon, buh ah telling yuh,
slavery eh done yet, yuh know. Education is
de onliest way outa slavery, so yuh better siddown
read yuh book.

2

After evening johnnie bakes, soursop bush tea
he sat in the orange glow of a pitchoil lamp
reading Nelson's West Indian Reader,
how that *little one-eyed, one-armed man*
hounded Villeneuve across troubled seas;
how under Sir Ralph Abercromby, Trinidad became
a British colony without sword and cannon fire.

But where was his grandmother's history?
Look for her history
in African cooking pots
simmering with food for the soul, blending
the bitterness of enslavement with a sweet
freedom of spirit to survive.

Look for her history
in the love chamber of the big house
on the Alexanders' cocoa plantation;
the creole ochre of her skin,
her body's lexicon of gestures,
the onomatopoeia of feelings:

Eh-heh? Buh eh-eh!
Ah-ya-hai, mama yo!

History waiting to be written
in a nation's first language.

SESTINA WID RUM

If yuh could pour a sestina in a bottle,
put some Caribbean culture wid it,
add *mountain dew* rum, shake it well,
mek it tasty to European taste,
stick a label: Caribbean Sestina Cocktail,
we could serve it at literary conventions.

People dey dance till dey drop. Conventions
would go, as if dey did drink a whole bottle
of cacapool rum; not de sort fuh cocktail.
Sestina wid rum! Yuh doh know yuh drinkin it.
It got de sunny, smoode nation language taste;
even curry goat and sestina go down well.

Critics say we like parrot. We imitate well.
Mimicking we do fuh irony. Conventions
we subvert, bending language to suit we taste.
Dat ting like water in ah unlabelled bottle
is we spirit, man. Authorities try to ban it:
Dis wild rum too strong fuh European cocktail.

Nation language in a sestina cocktail
we love; buh we could still speak English well.
Is always a question of our survival. It
have a ting dey call 'iamb', a convention,
a flavour in dey literary bottle;
buh rum sestina rhythm is more we taste.

We tief de dactyl, give it sugarcane taste,
mek it good fuh calypso an sestina cocktail.
English slang would say, *we gotta-lotta bottle*
to tro off we clothes an shake we body so well;
buh dis is we carnival culture convention;
is we language; yuh just have to accept it.

11

An man we really love dis sestina cocktail. It
so much better as a Caribbean taste.
Calypsonians as poets create new conventions,
dey challenge poetry dons to accept dis cocktail.
Fuh de sake of literature, dis is a well
of opportunity fuh freedom; not to bottle

up resentment, buh drink we sestina cocktail.
Man, we reshaping convention, creolising it well;
so, lehwe mix-up de new taste; pass de rum bottle.

YOU NOT A SOUCOUYANT

Granma, Granma
is not true,
is not true
you a soucouyant like Ma Joe
cause she ole like you.

Is not true
is not true;
Ma Joe, she ole like you
buh she dohn cook
coocoo an spicy callaloo
wid crab in it;

an besides, wen ah siddong close to you
yuh smell like cinnamon.
No soucouyant cud smell like dat.

Tell meh, Granma,
is it true?
Is not true
you ah soucouyant like Ma Joe
cause she ole like you.

Please tell meh Benny is a liar;
tell meh yuh dohn fly
like a ball of fire.

Well sonnyboy, coocoo and callaloo
is one of meh favourite food;
an ah do like a blazing fire.
Yuh know, every night ah dream about flyin.

Oh yes, yuh Granma is very, very special,
not a soucouyant like Ma Joe;
an ah telling yuh
dat's de gospel trute.

13

THE HOMELESS HEART

For Mamie, my Great Grandmother

The Yoruba taught Mamie to be strong.
At eighty she was quick on her feet;
in market crowds elbowed her way along,
demanded *langniappe* to make ends meet.

My mother was her only grandchild,
orphaned not long from toddlerhood.
She would brave hurricanes for her; denied
her nothing, indulged her every mood.

She was always my mother's counsellor
in marital disputes. My father
grew to abhor what her love stood for.
Knowing that this daughter-great-grandmother

thing could grow stronger and never die,
he threw great granny out, *tout bagai.*

INVOCATIONS

We ate our evening johnny bake,
drank sweet lime bud tea.

Before going to bed, we huddled
in the back-yard where a boldface moon
cast yellow shadows under the mango-vert tree.

Our story-telling summoned
the blood-sucking Loupgaroo,
La Jabless with her lethal coquetry,
shape-shifter Papa Bois, keeper of forests;

then, from some other dark place,
a jumbie-owl began its own story
in tremolo-ooo.
Who then was brave enough to scurry
past moon trembling shapes
to climb the wooden backdoor steps to bed?

*

Night's black
hung on a taut wire of silence.
Sleep did come, but with the cold sweat of nightmares:
my grandfather ghosted in dragging behind him
the threadbare rag doll of his spent libido.

He avoided the cold stares of the wife,
who a long time ago threw him out
when she caught him at it, again.

There at the front of the house, he stood
behind the barrier gate,
remote from her heart,
with the sins of the fathers
in the hollow of his eyes.

NANNY'S REINCARNATION

After the beating by plantation sun,
the silencing of the drums, night was comfort.
Your ancestral ways simmered in a pepperpot
in the dark, spiced with wild thyme, casareep.

Obeah was your faith.
You soothed monthly pains with zebapique,
drove evil spirits away
burning cacajab in coalpot fire.

A century later, you were Ma Trojedha
in a sick room, immersing an agued boy
in a washtub, sweet-broom Sargasso Sea.
You lashed him with the healing herb,
rubbed the fever out of him:

bring meh some sorf-candle,
salt and nutmeg, bay rum and matches.

The mixing done, you poured rum
and lit it: flame-blue tongues
licked and melted the ointment.

After the massage you wrapped him in a blanket.
The fever beaded his skin, soaked the bed.

He go be runninroun flyin kites tomorrow,
you, Ma Trojedha, said.

A RAINY, RAINY SEASON GULLY IN ROCKLEY VALE

1
For days it rained like the Bible
on Rockley Vale, where the Reverend Hosiah
rose in his pulpit, changed his accustomed rhetoric
to tumbling words on words of Brueghel pictures,
sinners roasting in the fires of hell.

His new apocalypse: *Inundation in silt-stink*
boiling flood waters wid all dem living creatures cursed
to crawl on their bellies. His message bounced
off the rafters in the Church of God chapel.
Take heed, I tellinyuh. Dis ent no ordinary rain.
Not natural de sky cud hol so much water. Gord
didn't sen dis rain to dousedong de fires of hell
dat yuh deserve. Dis is annoder hand of de Laard.
Is like ah second Noah flood – Yuh go drong! Yuh go drong!

2
But the indigo clouds gave way; and the sky
turned the colour of wash-tub water.
No waiting for a twig-bearing dove
from the Pigeon Hill mountain. We squelched through
Grandma Phoebe's acres to the gully's roaring rush,
breathed in the earth odour, saw tree roots exposed
in a dangling dance of turbulent river.

Gone was the whip-snake's track across the gully,
that young willow stretched from bushy bank to bank.
Gone the crayfish's *mauby*-coloured pools,
the oxbow arc of picnic sand, our impromptu fireside
on the gully's bank for breadfruit roasting.

Above the grumbling of the boulder-pushing water,
we thought we heard the Sabbath voice of the Rev. Hosiah.
Praise! Praise de Laard fuh his mercy. We safe now.
It was a warning. We safe now. Buhlet dem badjohn
an every good-fuh-nottin jamet wid dey bacchanal ways
take heed. Dey better stop de wining an dey liming
in broad daylight like daag. Hallelujah!

JUMBIE JAMBOREE

Tonight is jumbie jamboree
in Mucurapo Cemetery
and what you know,
there is rum, souse and coconut bread
and jumbie bawling to wake the dead!

Ah tell you, is true
dem jumbies making spree
drunk in that midnight cemetery,
and jumbie hugging and kissing jumbie
doing rude things in a decent country.

And when the band strike up a leggo,
boy, the music is hot-hot calypso,
just listen how the rhythm flow
as they dance and sing in harmony:

Back to back, belly to belly,
we don't care a damn
we done dead already;
back to back, belly to belly
in this jumbie jamboree.

SERIOUS TING CARNIVAL

Just in case yuh dohn notice,
I go tell yuh:

Every time is carnival
dey is always some man
who want to dress-up
like woman.

An gurl,
is no maga-maga woman either.
She always big-big wid a pillow
right down de back,
two cushions up front.

It mus be sometin important
he tryin to say.

Carnival is serious ting, yuh know.

THE JUMBIE BIRD ABROAD

Why here in these Pennine hills,
this windy, seepy landscape
of russet bracken and hardy heather, growing wild
like the zootie in Tobago's bush?

Are you that same jumbie bird
I glimpsed in a twilight, darkening
like stories told in the shadow of a sandbox tree?

Am I so steeped in mysteries
I see a jumbie in an English crow
foraging in the wild,
haunted only by the instinct to survive?

THE MAKING OF A MAROON

Slave spirits held my tongue.
I must not betray the dark rebellion
in my cutlass's keen blade.

Massa in his big house
with the hanging glass
of rainbow-glinting colours;

Massa with his painted teacup,
as fine as cocrico eggshell.

He did not see it coming:
the burning cane fields,
the disabled work-horses,
poison in the food.

I ran faster than Massa's rage, away
from the bull-pestle, stocks and manacle,
away to the mountains
where hatred brewed,
where cutlasses were whetted on stone.

BLOODY BAY TOBAGO

Reached by steep land
with tumbling speed of falling scree,
it lies in an empty sheltered gloom;
but from a fisherman's sea view
this nibbled coastline curves,
white sand like a gleaming sickle.

There is a rankness here of seamen's tales:
a death by drowning, lovers still locked together;
a beached carcass like a ribbed hull
of some sea monster eels picked clean.

It is here in a vermilion sunset
that I once heard the call: 'Baraaaaaacuuuudaaaaa.'
They return here again and again to glut
on memories of a feast
when the water in this bay turned red.

Lure of the Cascadura

A POEM FOR MY FATHER

You lived a peculiar independence,
you, the progeny of slaves
scarred with a history perpetrated
in killing cane fields.

I watched you,
amazed at your well-mannered poise.

Was this mute rage against them
who offered baubles as gems,
vinegar as water?

There were some
who thought you learned too easily
to hold your tongue between teeth,
to wear too comfortably in the sun's burning
your three piece suit.

There were others who greeted you
with a conditioned respect.
They looked up to you, called you, sir,
cowed by your cultivated Englishness.

Yet you took no vacations abroad.
You cobbled morning, noon and night,
work was a striding to your grave.
All you bequeathed was the memory
of your ways.

FOR THE ARAWAKS OF CU-MUCURAPO

Where are they now,
the Arawaks who discovered Columbus

blundering West to India
war dancing to tambourines off Punta Arenal?

Their spirits linger still
in Arawak limbo, a valley in Hispaniola.

They move in trees and stones
sepulchring Cu-Mucurapo,

where Sedeño once caught
the frightened white of their eyes in his cannon flash.

Where are they now,
these manioc eaters, children of Jacahuna?

Their middens speak:
broken phrases of discarded artifacts,

an Amerindian race
devoured by omnivorous history.

FRONTSIDE BACKSIDE

Frontside,
the usual façade for strangers
and officials carrying briefcases.

From the steps beyond the veranda
they turn away to cross the garden
spread like a wide summer skirt,
printed with red and yellow zinnias, intense marigold;

and beyond the white-washed wooden fence on guard,
they joined the hell-bent traffic, screened
with rolling dust of the Eastern Main Road, going
from Port-of-Spain to San Fernando.

Backside,
reserved for family and good friends:

Cheeky, weakling weeds testing their strength
on the tough, garden sugarcane;
careless stepping stones across the black mud
to the latrine, where the heated shit smell fought
valiantly the statutory DDT,
and beyond this, a wilderness of black sage and Christmas bush,
where the wilful, wayward fowls find a nesting place;
but this is mongoose country, and fowls have short memories.

After this pathless waste, the grief acre of graves
grieving west to the modest railway line with its galvanized halt.

Here on one side of the line, the blue crabs
are banking the mangrove mud at the mouth of their holes;

but beyond this point is the real test of friendship:
the swamp oozes to the desolate sea coast with no ships in sight.

ISLAND MUSE

I come with my pen
from Baptist Shouters,
candles burning on the edge of darkness
at the side of the road in limbo,
where repentance sings
in hallelujahs,
in amens,
in the clapping harmony of hymns.

I come with my pen
from the drum, drum
drumming Shango rhythms
in the tent of dancing sacrifices,
in the pulsing blood squirts of cocks' hearts.
From the drum, drum
drumming on calabash covered chicken,
drumming away death with Yoruba magic.

I come with my pen
walking the middle of the jumbie midnight road,
hair standing up, heart big in mouth,
clinging to 'our Fathers', 'Lord is my Shepherds',
avoiding dubious pools,
avoiding obeah big foot,
smelling cacajab,
walking backwards through front door.

I come with my pen
from where the jumbie 'buds' at midday
hoot, hoot, hoot from sandbox tree
and the dog-wailing death-song
suck the last breath of the ailing;
crapaud hopping into drawing room,

mirrors cracking suddenly,
wind coming from nowhere
blows out pitchoil lamps
and blessed candles.

I come with my pen
from cool green forest
where Papa Bois, bearded with vines,
protects the gouti, lapp and quenk;
where macajuel, like fallen-down tree trunk,
sleeps with belly full of cow.
Where mapepire zanana strikes
the deer-chasing dog,
while cigals trill for rain.

I come with my pen
from where the wily douens,
kidnappers of kiddies under full moon,
faceless, walking forward, backwards into bush;
from where Mama Malade is a naked baby
under midnight street lamp whimpering,
La Diablesse hiding her cow foot
under wide French petticoat,
Soucouyant and Loupgarou, balls of fire,
brightening roof tops before the sucking feasts.

I come long years with my pen
and island hauntings
from where my navel string tree
still grows.

LURE OF THE CASCADURA

Exiled under silver birch and conifers
I see the poui and immortelles blooming;

the mistle thrush sings,
but I hear the kiskadee,
Qu'est ce qu'il dit,
qu'est ce qu'il dit.

Blue crabs scuttle in mangrove mud
where this forest floor is a compost
of dead leaves;

that grey squirrel is no agouti
sniffing the air for hunters in rain forest;

I listen to the birch's sigh
and hear distant rain approaching;

pewah and pomme-arac
usurp the taste of peach and Cox's pippin;

but I have savoured the cascadura
spiced with legend and must return to die
where the scarlet ibis flame.

WEDDIN PARTY

Tonite Soucouyant and Loupgarou get married
buryingroun jumbies sing *here comes the bride*;
jumbie birds come from far and wide,
Papa Bois, La Diablesse,
- an we know how dem two like commesse -
all dem little moonlight douens,
in fact, de whole damn ban
join in de bacchanal.

Even Bacoo-Man come out he little bottle
and fly in from Guyana.

Soucouyant and Loupgarou so happy,
fuh a joke dey conspire
to join up dey ball-a-fire
an nite turn day,
jumbie music begin to play
an everybody dance a breakaway.

THE PARTING

After all these years
your blood drained face is still
cradled in coffin mauve.

You look so far away
lying there.

I see black serge suits
– brought out only for lodge and funerals –
startling the white lilies around you,
their death fragrance mixing
with odour of camphored wardrobes.

Eyes are raw red;
father a stranger in his guttural grief moans;
my brothers and sisters
all toddlers' eyes large with innocence.

This day is veiled with tears
as you leave me for the cold earth,
and I only nine.

DEY IS KIATS AN KIATS

Kiats in Englan!
Dey spoil, *oui*:
dey laugh and play
hide-an-seek wid mice;
buh lehme tell yuh someting,
in de Caribbean,
we different altogedder.

Frastart, we always hungry
– as real kiats should be.
Wen we huntin,
we fass like lightnin
ready fuh anyting dat move.

On de odderhan,
here in Englan kiat get fat
on tin food from supermarkit;
man, dey losin all selfrespeck:
dey dohn even begin to know
how to ketch mice;
an dey ha de brassface to believe
dey better dan we back home.

Yuh know wat I tink!
– I go tell yuh anyway –
because dey go to dem beauty salon
to get deself dollsup,
because dey geh deself sterelise,
dey tink dey modern an liberated,
eh heh, ah know wah ah talkin bout
ah tellin yuh,

I hear dem wid meh own ears:
dey call we Caribbean kiats

'primitive wild beasts',
well, dat mek meh laugh;
we so-called wild beasts
dohn en up in de vet all de time,
we live natural and healty,
free as a bird;
well, free anyway.

ENGLAN NO MUDDERCOUNTRY

Englan no muddercountry.
Ole West Indian 'istry book
was tellin lie: is white man
mamaguy.

Englan
no 'Land of Hope and Glory',
ask di so-called Black minority,
dey tell yuh a different story:

buh Englan
'Mother of the Free',
yeh, free to burn a Pak,
free to mug a Black,
is a fack.

Man, dis is National Front country,
wid aerosol-can graffiti:
'Gas the Blacks',
say di writin on di wall.

Here any Black man can carry
di collective identity:
wog, nigger, alien disgrace,
slum-maker, wife-stealer,
contaminator of di English race,
job-tief, sociological case,

an yu tellin meh
Englan mi muddercountry.
Cheups!

GODFATHER'S 'OLE TALK'

Everybody called him Godfather.
I once saw a portrait by Cézanne
of an old man just like him,
dappled with the colours of permanent summer.

Godfather sat at ease with his garnished tales:
how once he played cricket with Edward,
the Prince of Wales, when they were both young
and agile on a pitch in Tobago,
now somebody's sweet potato patch.

The memory of those gone days
passed through him like an earth's tremor,
and his eyes for a brief moment
lit up like a candlefly's.

He seemed glad for my company
and the present of Vat 19 rum from Trinidad.
He cried a little.

GRANMA'S SABBATHS

Woe to the breakers
of Granma's hymn-singing sabbaths,
to the blasphemers of her God-spell
cast to silence the wind's pea-pod rattling,
'bluchies' chattering in the hog plum tree,
cackling gol-eye sarah.

Granma's sabbaths,
always a sit-down breakfast:
cocoa tea, fry bakes and saltfish accra.

After breakfast, the clean-starched-linen-smell march
from Rockley Vale to any church in Scarborough.

'Dey's only one Gaard, and chuch is chuch,
praise de Laard', Granma used to say.

Then after service, Sunday school bible tales:
'Jonas in de whale belly, Daniel in de lion den'.

No work on sabbath day, but no play either.
'Johnieeeeeeee, haul yuh tail ere;
how many times ah tell yuh not to play
"stick-em-up" on de Laard sabbath.
Johnieeeeeeeee, wey yu dey, comere yuh little vagabon,
yuh come right ere befoe ah whip yuh backside
till it black and blue!'

JOURVAY

Foreday mornin
just round de corner.
Steelban
trobbin, trobbin,
trobbin in meh heart
beatin, beatin,
beatin in meh blood;

everybody winin-up,
jumpin, jumpin,
jumpin-up,
bottom to bottom,
breasts to chests,
belly to belly,
hands up down sideways,
all over de place;

and people sweatin,
sweatin fuh so,
waitin, waitin fuh six o'clock.
And when he cock crow on Lavantie Hill
and church bell ring,
ring, ringin out,
Jourvay break away.

We move out on de road,
and pan sweet sweet, ah tellin yuh;
everytin shakin, shakin,
shakin wid de riddum.
JOURVAY!

JUMBIE HEADMAN

(The announcer of death)

He lived unapproachable
at the heart of his stench;

armed with sharp thrust of eyes,
cutlass cradled in the crook of his arm.

With the brash obscenity of a carrion crow
he savoured the smell of death.

Before jumbie birds hooted,
before the *crapaud* in the drawing room,
before dogs howled at invisible presences,
before the mirror cracked on the wall,
this announcer of death came in the night,
Wake people, wake! Wake people, wake!

Three nights' walk away,
someone had died only seconds ago.

KITE WARDING OFF MAL YEUX

I know from my hovering height
there is something more to me
than my pretty cut of colours.

I rose on a breeze not strong enough
to ruffle duck's down.

Now I feel your heart beat through taut thread,
your desire to ride with me on the supple wind.

I am your will curved in 'coki-yea' bow and shaft,
in bright green and yellow tissue paper.

I changed your perspective at my height
warding off *mal yeux* with my aerial eye.

LOSS PROMISE LAN

Laard, Laard,
wah ah goin do now.
Look at me crosses.
Tell meh wey ah went wrong, meh Laard,
to en up in dis place.

Oh Laard ah fright'n
an feel so expose;
if yeye could knock meh doun ded,
ah would-a-be ded long time.

Wey ah doin in dis country, Laard?
Dey ehn no sun here to write home bout,
to top it all, meh skin gettin pale
ah tellin yuh, ah dohn feel right.

Dis ehn no Canaan lan, Laard,
Yam, eddoes, dasheen an sweet potato
dohn grown in back giard'n.
An ah cahn believe meh yeye,
here in Englan callaloo come in tin.

Yuh cahn go dong in de bush
after de rain stop fallin to pick up ripe mango.

Laard, Laard ah must-a-been blind:
back home in Tobago ah was livin all dat time
in de promise lan, right before meh eyeball
an ah didn't see it.

'MAN DED, MAN DEY'

Before Boysie gone an get hiself
knock down by a macktruck,
he livin in de rumshop all day Gord sen.

An wen sun climb down behind
dem mango tree, he come home stink ah rum,
singing at de top of 'is voice:
ain't no hidin place down 'ere,
he so drunk, he cahn get 'is clothes off.
Buh ah tellin yuh, meh dere, now he gone away,
man died, man dey.

An chile, dat's not all: he always climbin all over meh,
'is ting all wrinkle-up, hangin down
like dem dry banana leaf, not even a stiff dose of *bois brande*
could mek it stan up;
Oh Gord! Now Boysie gone away,
girl, man ded, man dey.

I give im a good wake, yuh know;
a-lot-a-soda biscuits an coffee, rum was flowin like water,
we sing plenty hymns, especially
'is favourite: 'Abide wid me'.

It was in de wake 'is pardner, Broko,
start givin meh de sweet-eye.
Well, chile, it didn't tek long,
now ah know wat I was missin.

Boysie gone away,
buh man ded, man dey.
We gettin married nex Easter,
before de chile born.

SKIN SKIN, YUH NA KNOW MEH

Soucouyant, Soucouyant,
ball of fire vampiring through the night,
I found your skin beneath a water barrel
        and salted it,
        and salted it;

                'Skin skin, is me, yuh na know meh,
                skin skin, yuh na know meh'.

No more banquets of blood,
no more purple rings
on my skin in the mornings;
no more chalk marks: crosses and noughts
on doors and windows to keep you away;
I found your skin beneath a water barrel
        and salted it,
        and salted it;

                'Skin skin, is me, yuh na know meh,
                skin skin, yuh na know meh'.

In daylight, you, an old woman leaning on stick,
shunned the chalk line across your path;
you raved and cursed
marking the next victim with blaze of your eyes.
Children taunted you:
        'Soucouyant, Soucouyant!'
But I found your skin beneath a water barrel
        and salted it,
        and salted it;

                'Skin skin, is me, yuh na know meh,
                skin skin, yuh na know meh'.

THE CARIB BEAN

The Carib bean
green greed
of the French,
of the English,
of the Dutch,
of the Spaniards.

Staple provisions
for conquistadors
trekking to
El Dorado,
trekking
through
'carne',
carni-
vorous jungle
to Montezuma's
headgear of suns
burning,
burning up,
burning the flesh,
igniting
their gold lust,
acrid odours
all the way
to the courts
of Spain.

Carib bean
fed nations of Europe.
They claimed
it went well with everything,
preferred with Arawaks

roasted in flames
of Carapichaima,
of Cu-Mucurapo,
in the flames
of Arima, Chaguanas
and Couva,
before the slaves,
canned in their oozes,
shipped West,
labelled Yoruba,
Ashanti, Coromantee,
brothers of Cudjoe.

So many died:
Africans,
Amerindians,
currency for the Carib bean.

The Sun Rises In The North

AIYO! AIYO!

I saw him purse his lips,
heard him whistle a breeze for flying.

In the answering gust
I lifted from his quivering thread of fist.

Sun proud in orange and yellow,
I serpentined to an eagle height,
razor-zwilled tail of blades
and slivers of green glass
lust-glinting to dive, to cut loose
my nearest enemy.

And when I dived
my tail was a thread slasher;

aiyo! aiyo!
to the enemy's dying drift
towards tangled green graves
of faded kites.

AT ANTOINE'S BARBER SHOP

There was a time, swivelled to its full height,
I still needed a wooden box in the barber's chair.

I was growing to the decreasing swivel of a man:
If only yuh dead mudder could see you now, Antoine said.

I listened to the rapid scissor talk and barber shop debate:
Man, Sugar Ray could box fuh so!
He better than your Joe Louis, any day.
I tellin yuh, HE was a sweet sweet mover.
Joe Louis flat footed, cahn dance like ole Sugar.

And when the razor came out unfolded,
slapping itself keen on the leather strap,
I held my breath, stopped listening
till soap suds were wiped away.

Brilliantined, talc powdered,
unscathed with short back and sides,
1 left the barber shop shadow boxing.

BOBOLEE

Good Friday,
like holy Granma Sundays.

Baptist shouters in long white cotton
walked like in funerals,
ringing bells,
singing hymns.

We waited for hen to cackle.
When we found her egg
we put the white in a drinking glass,
left it in Good Friday sun,
watched our future appear in pictures;

then the Judas rag doll,
as big as a man,
was dragged through the streets.

Every beating boy with a long stick,
'bolee, bolee, beat the bobolee,
bolee, bolee, beat the bobolee',
beating towards the big fire waiting
for Judas in the stone quarry.

FLYING A BUNTING FOR MANHOOD

By some strange coincidence
Reverend Cumberbatch chose
Corinthians one, verse eleven
for his Sunday preaching text:

'When I was a child, I spoke like a child
when I became a man, I gave up
childish ways'.

That day of all days,
with me proud as a young yard cock
in my first long pants.

That day I held my nose high,
higher than when I found my first secret fob.

Fists deep in side pockets,
nobody could call me mannish.

With impunity I was able to hang a hankie
from my back pocket, flying like a bunting.

There was manly substance about me
in those long pants styled like Rochester's.

That Sunday night my father, a little embarrassed,
gave me a book covered with brown paper;
'A book every young man should read,' he said.

MYTH MAKER

For this green water fowl
every dry season is ritual
death in the scorched gully.

Yet, a wet season ago, it was
a green flash splash-landing
in deep water where the gully bends;

or in its spindled strut
broke the shallow stillness,
coiled spring of its neck wound back
to strike at guppy and crayfish.

Its death is a stink now
from a feather-bag of bones;
but life will flesh it up again
for another wet season.

TELLIN STORIES

Teacher mus tink
I am a chupidie;
she tellin me bout cow
jumpin over de moon.

Dat is mamaguy.
I wonder how
a cow could jump so high!

But dat not de only lie!
How bout dis dish
dat run way wid a spoon.

I expect dat soon
she go talk bout some fish
in shirt and tie
talking to a snail
bout somebody steppin
on he tail.

NO APPLES IN EDEN

There were no apples in Eden,
only sapodillas ripening among
bougainvillaea and frangipani.

The serpent was a mapepire snake
in the sapodilla tree, observing
how God drugged Eve with deep sleep,
plucked an organ from her body,
made it into Adam.

This snake with guile in smooth slithers
curled around Adam's thighs, stirred his desires,
sweetened his tongue with words
as delicate as the flavour of sapodillas,
made a seducer of him.

And when Eve uttered Adam's name
at the acme of her pleasures,
Eden shook under God's footsteps.

Oh the discovery of shame!
They covered their nakedness
with blooms of bougainvillaea.
The mapepire hid in a balisier flower.

Behind the Carnival

GRANDPA DOLPHUS

When Grandpa Dolphus
pushed car-tyre sandals off,
rubbed apart stuck toes, you knew
he'd come in to stay
till next day when rum shop opened.

When he reached for the tin of twist,
trawled pockets for his sweet pipe,
you knew rigmaroles were coming without
the crick-crack-monkey-break-he-back-
on-a-piece-a-pommerac endings.
He swore every single word was gospel.

He told about under silk-cotton and sandbox trees
where jumbie happenings bristled his hairs
like Grandma's scrubbing brush.
How he made the sign of the cross, ran off
not looking back, not petrifying into salt.
He told how giant forms held the moon
blocked the road, sucked his breath
till he turned about to save his life.

We heard those tales so many times before.
Only the dog gave its dumb attention:
It rolled its eyes in the direction
its listening head should be.

When Grandpa Dolphus pushed Columbus,
our don't-care-a-damn cat, off his lap
you knew his pipe had burnt itself out
like his tales;
but only for that night.

UNCLE CYRIL

Que hay!
A call from across the road.
Shambling towards me, Uncle Cyril,
our family sailor, adventurer
down the Spanish Main, bent
like a question mark
to disguise his six feet four.

Que hay!
El Dorado glinted in his grin.
Hands weathered like good leather
reached out. Carelessness hung about him,
tilted his hat, gave him that look
Grandma called roguish.

His pockets hung heavy with coins.
Buy sweeties, but don't be lickerish.
Save some fuh yuh brodda an sisters.
How is yuh granma?

Uncle Cyril had made and lost
a fortune trafficking live stock
to the market in Port-of-Spain,
fishing in his half-owned boat
for anchovies and jacks.

Years later, his seafaring over,
my father found him
consumed by bush lore in a forest
near Charlotteville in Tobago
guarded by a vicious sow,
a butting goat and a parrot screeching:
Que hay! Que hay!

BEHIND THE CARNIVAL

In the beginning was carnival:
the pulse that animated the germ in the soup,
made sperm a triumphant amphibian,
stirred seed to shoot, burned green
in every tree and herb. The earth
became woman's sister
and men hid their awe behind masks,
shaped wood and clay into their fear
behind the carnival.

Behind the carnival
awe turned to dancing; the moaning
was not wind through trees
when lust was innocent
behind the carnival.

Behind the carnival
African gods came out of stones,
gave power to the throbbing drums.
Yokes and barracoons could not destroy
deep harmonies of their chanting
behind the carnival.

Behind the carnival
the whipping voice drove slaves
from beds, each one a flambeaux-bearer
coursing with a strength to survive,
dousing cane fields burning up the night
behind the carnival.

Behind the carnival
was a camboulay of dancing torches;
Jabmolasi cavorting, a different fire
in his loins; but that freedom
was as seed-cotton blown in hurricane
behind the carnival.

Behind the carnival
Ma Jake weeps in her chicken pelau,
remembering her daughter who danced
too long in the rain, caught pleurisy
was buried seven days later
behind the carnival.

Behind the carnival
Carmen, saving to play mas,
rakes her mind before coal-pot fire
trying to figure out how to make ends meet
behind the carnival.

Behind the carnival
Boysie argues with his wife,
mother of nine hungry picknies:
He must follow in his father's footsteps
playing midnight robber
even if it's the last thing he does
behind the carnival.

Behind the carnival
no Devil Band for Sharkie this time:
He was practising his wining-up too close
to a woman jamet; he is in hospital now,
balls kicked in
behind the carnival.

Behind the carnival
jumbie owls screech.
They see what no masquerader sees:
the portent in Bad-behaviour sailors' dance,
las lap we go beat massa-massa,
las lap we go beat massa-massa
behind the carnival.

Behind the carnival
the dragon menaces;
but he is chained by steel
tempered in the hell of sugar plantations
and must learn to dance calypso.
'Hold the dragon,
hold the dragon,'
behind the carnival.

BLACK TRIANGLE

It hovered above my head, a black patch
bristling like a dog-scared cat.

Even when a hand came down, scratched it
in the small window twilight
of the room, it remained silent.

I wanted to reach out and touch it,
but something held me back.

I knew it from somewhere,
that mouth stretched to the limit
and my being forced out
into blinding light, deafening noise.

I lived again the musk of closeness, the touch
of a body-warmed chemise,
a nuzzling softness and sweetness
to stop me crying.

CRACK IN THE PEDESTAL

Grave diggers
drenched in the rain
prepared a place for you.

They were drinking rum
from a broken skull,
protection from
the wandering souls
of bodies they dug up.

Years after that rain
and eyes red with tears,
I come back to a mound of earth
among spring green
where my happy childhood
was buried still
clinging to you.

I stand here wondering who
kept your grave free of weeds.

FATHER'S PHOTOGRAPH

After thirty three years I am back,
goose fleshed before your photograph.

You stand feet planted square,
straight eye contact; remind me
of that day we stood on the wharf,
words clogged with mutual admirations,
regrets, hopes, things slipping away.

We embraced – we must have.
I boarded the launch which took me
to the *Venezuela* anchored in deep water,
my eyes clinging to you as it sped away.

Half a mile out and I could still see
your white hankie in the breeze like a flag.

Now, even in this faded photo,
I see the firm set of your lips
telling so much of your struggle
against all odds. Once when I was twelve
you set me down, explained away
the concept of failure.

I remember the way your shoulders shook
when you laughed; your stubble on my cheek.

You died on a day when I lay cold
in an English town conjuring pictures
of a Trinidad in fruit-ripening sun.

Yesterday I drove to the burying ground
in Barataria, was told they had to dig you up
to make room for another.

JUMBIE BIRD

In my country
night is a hunting day:
I see where rodents run
and my wings cut the darkness
in a sharp swoop.

Blood has no colour in the night;
only the warm, sticky taste
of flesh ripped.
Death is familiar as food.

I see the sun
long before it tints the sky.
Then, homing in
to my silk-cotton perch

where a fragment of night
is caught in a cluster of leaves,
I close my eyes, drift into dreams,
slide down a beam of light
to some place where death sits
heavy on the ailing.

Three times I hoot.
Midday sees me sleep-flying,
casting shadows
on a house of grief.

LANDING ON CRUSOE'S ISLAND

The sea sloped steeply as the plane banked,
began its panoramic sweep down.

Tobago from this height was no larger
than a dark green postage stamp.

Our quick descent telescoped the green,
magnified it to cultivated fields,
trees spattered with blossoms, bright birds.

In a field embroidered with furrows
a scarlet ibis flaunted its landing skill.

We landed with a bump, sped sea-ward
down a runway, veered at the last minute;
taxied to our designated parking.

I stepped out of the plane
and into glaring heat.
Instinct was to run seek out a cool place.

'Home, this is home,' squawked a corn bird
above the boom and wash of the sea
always never far away.

NEWS BREAKERS

His was the house scowling
under the stinkin toe tree,
the flower garden with a rabble
of weeds jostling for air.

They held back, afraid to enter.
How would they tell Ma Chac Chac?

They felt close to him then,
remembering his school-yard fame
as 'pincher Jack'. He was snot taster,
a long range spitter,
expert saliva bubble-blower.

He was the boy whose mouth watered
peeling dry scabs off healing cuts.

Once he out-ran Mr. Elder's mad dog;
not even the weight of stolen mangoes
stopped his leap to safety.

But this time his leap
was a splintering of bones.
The car never stopped.

TERRA-ANIMUS

There is something
in this soil,
where sugar cane grew for centuries,
that eyes can't see,
or fingers feel, that
you cannot hear or smell:

something unspeakable
that made a history
some still suffer with,
others choose not to write about,

thinking, perhaps, that words propagate
a life of questions, a relentless struggle
for answers.

There is something
in this soil
more than the humus
of dead slaves.

THE RACONTEUR

(For the Midnight Robber)

From shadows under sandbox tree
I heard spirits' voices,
silvery whisperings:
how in the beginning
the serpent
was a man-snake mapepire.

And after tricks with his tail,
he found a place to hide
among balisier flowers.
His fish-rankness spoiled their fragrance,
stiffened their silken orange flames.

Tales were told of owl and blackbird,
how they challenged the serpent's wiles.
He hexed them into jumbie birds,
harbingers of death.

All this occurred on the eighth day,
the Caribbean archipelago
a solid gem
before God's furious love
shattered it into a necklace of jades
strung between North America
and South America.

THE RETURN

Welcome is a blast of hot air
like a cuff in the face.
(Thirty three years is a long time.)

I too too-toolbay, can't kneel down
to kiss the soil like a good son.

Walking from the plane
my footsteps echo on the tarmac
like the day I was eager to leave.

I so too-toolbay, I can't think
of searching the Lavantille hills for the sapling
nourished by my navel string.

It must be a big tree now,
and, like an indulgent mother,
spoiling corn birds, giving its limbs
to their hanging nests.

And where is the old nursery school
on George Street in Port of Spain,
shuttered and locked against rioters
back in 38 when Charlie King
was burnt alive in a Southern oil field?

Where it gone, Marine Square with cassia,
poinciana and couples strolling?
It's now a bargaining trot along a chain
of ramshackle Rasta boutiques.

But still the smell of energy, the exuberance
of words, colourful
as Assyrians' fabric stores on Charlotte Street,
the urge to spree still burning
unruly as flambeaux in wind;
the calypso heartbeat
in the way the body moves.

WHAT A WAY TO GO

A sky the colour
of weathered galvanize
was not the burial day
he often joked about
between shots of rum
in the Black Cat Bar.

Coffin sealed
in his Sunday best,
quiet, first time ever,
he led the way
in a tasselled hearse
relatives closest behind,
then good friends
staccato of heels in the
hushed street.

Women remembered
his dancing hips,
gold-teeth smile,
how he loved a bacchanal.

Pass de rum, Jacko;
Lehwe fire one fuh Toby.
He woulda like dat.

That night
wake was good:
whe-whe in the yard,
all fours in candle light,
soda biscuits

with steaming coffee
and all the while,
the grief-wailings
disharmonising with
Rock of Ages,
Abide With Me.

He died as he lived;
except that a tom cat
has nine lives.
Toby had only one
too old for sleeping out.
Rumour had it
she was so spent
she couldn't
push him off.

Voices From A Silk-Cotton Tree

HAUNTINGS

When flesh was their home
they were driven by a nameless energy
into fields and forests of literature,
blind to the pitfalls of words.

They hoped
glimpses of poets' lives
embalmed in their verse
would inspire their own;
but the searching *was* their poetry.

They are at odds now with the tangible.
Their presence is the chill in sun-lit places.
Their knowledge is beyond the reach of metaphor.
They have no words but their hauntings,
darkening silk-cotton and sandbox.

THE ADOPTION

1

They tossed you three times over her.
She lay plugged with cotton wool,
cushioned in mauve satin,
lilies cold white on her embroidered breasts.

Afterwards, I looked at your blank face
and knew you were elsewhere with your pain.

Last night, through the rattle of rain,
it was not an owl I heard;
yes, live your tears and let me be
your mother now.

2

In the gloom he lay on his back
under her canvas cot,
feeling her body's heat.
He tried to match his breathing to hers.
He dared not touch, hands skimming
where canvas bulged.

In that close space
he shifted for comfort,
felt her shape against his knee.

3

Stop the giggling!
Don't excite yourself.
Besides, you are old enough now
to put your own clothes on.
And I must tell you,
I was the sister your mother never had.

FARDA

Meh farda was a man
who save his wuds,
his shakin larf fuh Christmas
and weddin parties
wen shots of Vat 19,
sweetened with prunes,
put commas, never full stops
in stories he share wid meh uncles;
an after every chaser,
larf buss out,
larf buss out.

Every Sunday
meh fada was a fo-day mornin poitique
in Port-of-Spain market.
He pay fuh his cress an crab
wid patois and ole-tork;
an fuh *langniappe*,
he lef wid annoder bunch ah cress;
he lef de vendor, tut-tuts shakin wid she larf.

Ah Lyons, yuh really have a sweet mout,
yuh really have a sweet, sweet mout.

Every day fuh years an years
meh farda ride he bike, Josephine,
to mek shoes in de city,
to stanup by he counter
shapin shoe leather
fuh farmers wid yam foot.
An doh ah didn't know it at de time,
de veins in he legs
was knitting varicose knots
fuh future pain.
Wen dey did topple im into bed,
'is obeah, is obeah,' de people said.

FATHER'S UNMARKED GRAVE

Ever since that jumbie bird
with stagnant-pool eyes bustled in,
stirred up the settled dust,
Father, I dream of you:

I dig the darkness
under a silk-cotton tree,
disturb your bones
which the earth claimed with ochre;
and I feel the yearning-for-a-hug love,
a stubble-against-toddler's-cheek love.
I search the weather map of your face,
see dark clouds gathering.

The day Mother died
you hid behind the bedroom door
confiding to the gloom.
But I heard
your belly-sound of grief,
felt tears inside me,
lost my firm ground.

NOT EVERY OLD WOMAN IS A SOUCOUYANT

That rheum-eyed woman,
with rough-dry skin
tottering on the pain of arthritis,
is butt for ragamuffins playing
away from their mothers' licking strap
and stinging tongue.

Over their doors, the horseshoe;
rice heaped a spell on doorsteps;
noughts and crosses in white chalk
construct magic barriers.

But that old woman has a doting grandchild
who calls her Mamie.
Sea moss, cooked to a jelly,
swivelled in hot milk and sugar
is her favourite drink;
not blood.

A ROOM IN THE CITY, 1938

We lived on Queen Street
near the market-heart of Port-of-Spain
with its odours of over-ripe fruit
and ground provisions, open street gutters.

We squeezed and bumped around
in an apartment partitioned
by my father into a cobbler's workshop.

The only window faced onto the street.
It was shuttered against the maco's eyes.
Daylight made a stealthy entrance;
and what you couldn't see in the gloom
was best left alone. Murmurings in dark corners
were an introduction to jumbie stories,
soucouyant and La Jabless of later years.

My father was hunched
at his cobbler's bench, visions focused
with an Old Testament faith,
plying awl and waxed hemp, stitching soles
in the incandescence of a carbide lamp.

My mother mothered behind a folded screen
in a space not big enough to laugh in.
Life for me was lived in a four poster bed
with brass knobs, some small and perfectly
round for marble pitching.

BREAKFAST SHED AND PEPPER

1

While city people still hugged the fusty warmth
of bedrooms, deaf to the yard-cock's fanfare,
Stevedores refuelled on fried king fish, bakes
and greasy cocoa-tea in the Breakfast Shed,
a place of many kitchens a stone-pelt away
from big boats moored to Port-of-Spain quay.

These muscled, ebony men saw their mothers
through the steam of pots.
They knew that overnight king fish had revelled
with thyme, hot Scotch bonnet pepper and shadow beni.
They knew that overnight the spirits of ancestors
had come to taste, to bless flavours of survival.

2

These days the Breakfast Shed draws
a motley crowd, like fowl to a feeding back-yard:
retired civil servants, septuagenarians to a man
and buddies now, make a shit-talk-and-food *lime*,
give fatigue, *mauvais-langue* old bosses
who barred their way up the ladder.

Executives in the flush of business youth,
short sleeves and Trini-island pride, tuck tie ends
away from cow heel soup, coocoo and callaloo,
their maco-talk sharper than the pepper sauce.

These days Europeans come, not to plant a flag,
or for Montezuma's gold, but the Midas sun.
The untanned enter slowly. They linger
over the patois-shouted menus;

cooks are patient:
... *An above all, mine de peppersauce.*

The well-tanned bee-line to their favourite kitchens,
order stewed king fish in Solomon-ah-gundy sauce,
rice and peas, mauby or sorrel to put out fires
raging in their throats.

PINK KIMONO

Never knew her name,
but I can still see her standing
in the doorway of her small apartment,
a pink kimono like a cascade of silk
from narrow shoulders,
large wet eyes, a skin of pale yellow ochre,
and paler still where kimono fell away
from a small breast.

How like a delicate water-colour she looked,
hugging her wasp waist and holding back
an escaping smile.

Just before pitchoil lamps were lit
and coconut vendors put match to flambeau,
her sweet-men came: the sagaboys
with zoot suits and hats rakish over eyes.

From time to time, the bacchanal rhythm
with bottle-an-spoon. Everybody was a maco then:
complained about the ruction,
stared at her silks and gold bracelets.
More in de motar besides de pestle,
the neighbours say.

NAVEL STRING OF POETRY

1

I searched that misty place of memory,
found my navel-string tree of poetry:

I am back in blue-grey city dawns;
coconut vendors plying their trade
on street corners, odours of green coconut
freshly cut and the *pièce montée* of donkey's dung,
green as wet season grass. The black tom
stalking pigeons on the roof
of the Chinese tea shop on Queen Street.
The market with its ceiling gothic
in wrought-iron and glass, its earthy smells
of home-grown crops and sweat of crowds jostling;
its echo of voices like rain on a galvanize house-top.
One block away, busses are rattling out of George Street depot,
pungent with exhaust fumes, engine oil and hot metal,
going East to Tunapuna, San Juan, Sangre Grande, Arima.

2

The Eastern Main Road is a deluge of traffic,
currents flowing in opposing directions.
Taxis pirate for trade with *bravé danchez* skill, and most days
a dead dog left swelling, ready to burst in the sun.
In this drama of speed and pollution,
the safest place is the gallery at the house-front.
Back-yard the mind senses metaphor, records
the noiseless riot of sweet broom, vervine and shandilay,
man-better-man, love vine and caccachat.
Here is where zandolies play and kiskadee
and sici-yea keep an eye on the bird-hunting cat.

3

Before words in syntax, the image.
Every pillatree holding up the house, every book margin,
every wall under threat: drawings made with
the charred remnants of the coalpot.
For colour, the spectrum of zennias,
chalk stones of yellow ochre, red-brown and grey
unearthed by the new-road tractor.
The scent of exposed earth
was *bois brande* to my libido:
drawings were rampant,
but not yet the budding of words.

4

Pleurisy, on the wings of the jumbie bird,
came, sat for seven days on my mother's forehead,
then took her away. I could not recognise
the cold mauve tint of her face, nor her stillness
among the living white lilies.

Years later on a dirt track in Tobago,
the feudal neighbour found me beating grief
into the ground, mouthing words only the earth understood.
She called a truce, spread the alarm across the cactus fence.

'Yuh callin yuh dead mudder spirit on me,'
my grandmother bawled.

HAULING IN THE SEINE

With each rhythmic grunt
the fishermen haul you in.
Spilled out on moon-soaked sand
you are sea harvest now, bewilderment
fixed in your lidless eyes,
gills sucking emptiness.

Fishermen celebrate. They blow
staccato harmonies on conches
calling the fish-tea cooks.

Like night gulls they come in a clamour,
brandishing tin-pans and calabashes.
Before the sun comes up
they will feast on fish-tea.

Some green fig, onion, ah squeeze
ah lime, some thyme an a Scotch bonnet pepper
drop in whole fuh flavour.
Is good fuh de brain.

SHOOTING STARS OVER FARMERS' FIELDS

That summer I wish you were with me
tasting the succulence of that roadside peach
as sweet as any pommerac.

And if that summer you were with me
to gaze at stars shooting
over farmers' fields in Normandy,
how your breasts would have heaved
on a wishing sigh, those stars
no match for your eyes.

I wish you here now far from that summer
observing how this chilled spring breeze
worries the cherry blossoms
in a garden across the street;

then we could sit believing
there is a sun somewhere above
this slapdash wash of grey
and hear the blackbird with its wistful song.

Lightning Source UK Ltd.
Milton Keynes UK
26 October 2009

145434UK00001B/6/P